The concise concepts of modern management   prof .*George Fayol* F-A-ALO

management and its various magazines in order to come up with a short result and concepts that lead to excellence and innovation and the ability to conclude and solve problems For difficulties as well as acquiring intellectual, administrative, technical and human skills in dealing in the administrative environment.

For this was the development of this book in my point of view is an imperative and I was wish to find such a short and useful book in my the beginnings of the process or educational, so I decided to put these concepts and i shortened them and tried hard to pick the useful from them so that everyone comes out with the benefit and the least effort and also the concept My work meets the needs of working in institutions, companies and organizations.

Prof. *George Fayol* F-A-ALO

The concise concepts of modern management   prof .*George Fayol* F-A-ALO

Business Management

Business administration is a science of economics with its own foundations and rules that coordinates production elements, such as manpower, capital, and management, a science that uses available resources, and employs them in a particular project, institution or organization, and these resources are used in the best possible cases. In terms of cost, quantity, quality and the right time, to reach their desired goals.

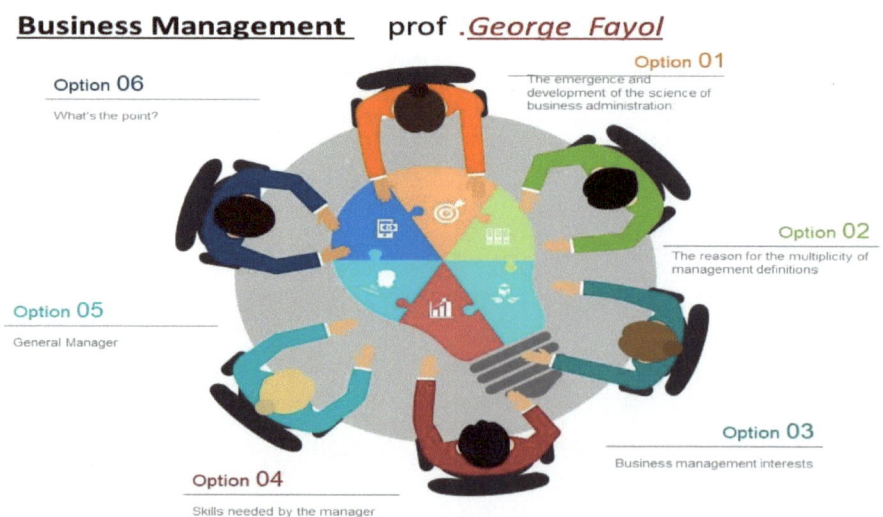

The concise concepts of modern management   prof .*George Fayol* F-A-ALO

Introduction

The importance of business management to society is constantly increasing, taking into account the technological development and the development of life in general, because management is the backbone of life because of the urgent need to make informed decisions to achieve the desired goal.

 As management is key to progress, focusing on the characteristics of success and prosperity of the business is positively reflected in the consolidation of the values and traditions of work, effort, respect for time, development of free thinking and responsibility.

The success of businesses and companies is mainly due to the presence of capable, strong, understanding , the nature of their tasks and actions, and conscious of the surrounding environment.

Therefore, the main task of management is to get the entire organization to aim for outstanding achievement through the best development of all resources.

The concise concepts of modern management   prof .*George Fayol* F-A-ALO

If we look at our daily lives, management is practiced first on a personal level through the management of one's living expenses, and on the other hand, management is applied at the collective level through the practice of various types of businesses for administrative activities.
 management has a place in all the activities of our daily lives.
So management in general is the cornerstone of every business.

Author's Word

This book is in your hands to illustrate the management concepts in a concise and simplified way through our experience in the field of business management over ten years of continuous experience.
And also through what we have learned in our scientific life in the field of business administration and I have been keen to choose all that is necessary and useful and needs the learner or who wanted to go into the principles of

The concise concepts of modern management   prof .*George Fayol* F-A-ALO

The origins and development of business management science:

Business management science originated in the late 19th century, with most of its models, research, schools and applications developed in the United States of America, and its development was carried out by American scientists of origin. It is said that Frederick Taylor is the first to applying this flag in 1903, known as the father of scientific administration, and has a big and clear effect in this field. Also The French scientist Henry Faule, who also had a clear fingerprint in business management science in 1916. Business management science is based on several bases and theories that make it an existing science in itself. Some of these foundations remain unagreed, resulting in the absence of a single view of the concept of management in a scientific or technical sense, and hence the multiplicity of definitions of business management.

Multiple and different management definitions

Many of the definitions of management science are that each scientist of management defined management according to his or her own scientific and practical background.

Among the most prominent of these definitions are:

First definition:
A set of activities that are associated with each other in order to implement effective control over its functionality.

Second definition:
These are the processes that are applied to activate people and things within the working environment, leading to the successful achievement of the required objectives.

The third definition, which is most appropriate in my view (important):

Business management is the process of achieving the goals set by utilizing available resources according to a specific approach and specific work environment.

Business Management Interests

The Department is concerned with planning, organizing, employing, directing, controlling and managing organized resources to achieve the objectives of the establishment.

the goal

The concise concepts of modern management   prof .George Fayol F-A-ALO

What are the goal ?

The goal is the end result we seek to achieve or reach.

The goal can be achieved by exploiting resources.

these resources are:

1- man 2- money 3- machines 4- material

5- market

6-management 7- time 8- information's

The General Manager

The General Manager

The General Manager is the person who directly controls all parts of the company or institution through the authority he owns and who forms the link between the facility and employees and its own objectives, because he is the primary responsibility for the tasks related to the course of the work for his sufficient experience in the proper management principles.

The Director General is therefore pursuing the implementation of the key management processes in the facility he manages best and most successfully through his experience and skills.

The skills a manager needs

The manager needs the skills to perform the management activity and these skills that should be available in the manager on a go

1. Intellectual skills

2. Humanitarian skills

3. Technical skills

4. Management skills

Intellectual skills: (Solving problems _ Conclusion _ Connecting matters).

Human skills: (Art of dealing with the business environment - attraction policy by good behavior).

Technical skills: (knowing how to deal with the computer).

Administrative skills: (Time management, meeting management, labor pressure management, negotiation, communication art).

The most important qualities of a successful manager

In any organization, the manager must have the characteristics of a successful leader:

1. Planning, monitoring and monitoring of all matters of the organization, whether small or large, by selecting the competent, experienced and responsible persons for each sector or department of the organization, and giving the appropriate powers to the heads, as no one can override laws or make decisions without relying on reviews, examinations and research.

The concise concepts of modern management   prof .*George Fayol* F-A-ALO

2. The vision of a successful manager is to have the ability to have a future vision and a right vision for his company in the future, setting a set of goals and factors to be achieved after a period of time, because a successful manager has specific, clear, and uninspiring goals. It has the ability to explain and simplify its objectives in a proper manner with a view to their implementation by its staff.

3. Consultation It is well known that any decision concerning the affairs of the institution is a priority for the manager, but it is important to keep away from despotism in his opinion, so that he should consult with him, and study all proposals and studies submitted to him seriously until the proper and correct decision is reached, Because advice makes the manager aware of things that are missing or not known about them.

The concise concepts of modern management   prof .*George Fayol* F-A-ALO

4. Transfer of experience to employees, it is supposed that experience and competence make the manager rise to his position and position in the organization or company, It would therefore be preferable for the manager to give his staff the information and expertise necessary to improve the performance of their functions, The work index is raised through some lectures and meetings.
5. That the role of the manager is the example to be followed in the organization or company, it is not reasonable for the manager to impose a set of instructions and laws within the organization and he is not committed to it or violates it. If there was a set of powers which the Director would be given to him only, it would be better to clarify them with transparency and tranquility.

Functions of the Director-General

The concise concepts of modern management   prof .*George Fayol* F-A-ALO

The duties of the Director General are all the responsibilities and duties incurred within and outside the boundaries of his company, and He must ensure that they are carried out correctly, both within the company and thus contribute to the implementation of management processes, Or outside, which reflects a positive image of the company in front of other companies, and in front of customers in particular and the community in general.

The most important tasks of the Director-General is what follows

- Supervising all day-to-day activities and operations in the company by continuously monitoring them.
- Ensure that you implement the best strategies that ensure continuous growth in your business environment.
- set goals for all tasks, measure the success of performance in implementing them, and follow up their reports.
- Attention to monitoring the work of executives, department heads, and supervisors of different businesses.

- Search for the best functional programs that can be successfully applied within the corporate environment.
- To seek to link the products and services provided by the company, with the nature of the targeted customers in the community.
- Interest in recruiting qualified staff, who contribute to professional development in all functional areas.
- To issue final decisions on major projects and development plans that will be implemented.
- Handle all employees of the company, and hear and motivate them to participate in meetings to identify achievements and challenges.
- Representing the company at local, regional and international conferences and meetings.

The Director-General Challenges

The general manager in the business environment faces a range of challenges, which he must deal with efficiently to overcome its negative impact, among the most important of which are:

- Confront the financial crises that may affect the company within a certain period of time, by trying to get out of them with the least possible losses.

The concise concepts of modern management   prof .*George Fayol* F-A-ALO

- Demonstrate all corporate strategies correctly for all managers so they can in turn transfer them to employees.
- Search for investments that are beneficial to the company and choose from them, which will help to preserve the future of the business.

Public Administration

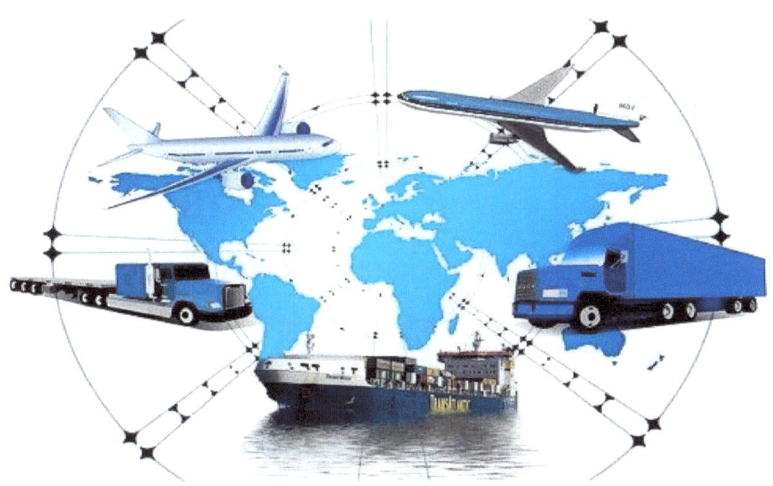

The concise concepts of modern management   prof .*George Fayol* F-A-ALO

Definition of public administration
Tasks that help exploit all available components to reach the target with the minimum time and cost.
The General Administration includes all operations that contribute to the proper continuity of the business.

Administrative levels
Management is generally divided into three levels of administration, namely:

Senior management level:
It is the level of public administration of enterprises and companies, and it also includes the department of the board of directors of large, multinational or branch organizations, which is considered to be the main control of all indirect administrative operations. Or that need direct authority to apply and implement them in accordance with the provisions, rules and instructions that will help to achieve the objectives that are successfully required.

Intermediate management level:

It is the level that contains enterprise and corporate branch managers, or a group of managers who are in charge of controlling operational processes, which are approved by senior management after being introduced at public meetings at the enterprise level, This level of management in some establishments also includes department heads and supervisors.

Minimum management level:

The level of secondary managers who are keen to implement the instructions and plans proposed by middle management under the guidance of senior management, including heads of staff or workers, and observers of executive movements, such as warehouse secretaries.

administrative pyramid

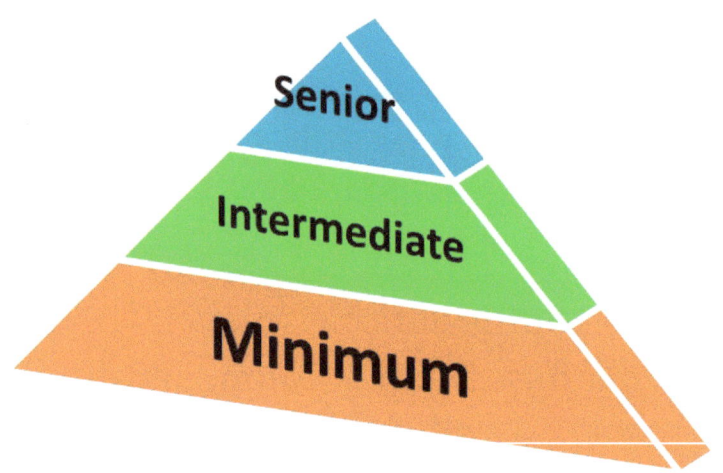

The functions of each department of administrative pyramid

Senior Management Functions:

1. Planning

2. Organize

3. Policy development

4. Setting general goals

5. Strategy Development

6. Consider the organization as one unit

Functions of the Central Administration:

The functions of the Central Administration are to translate objectives and policies into plans and programs.

Minimum Management Functions:

Supervise follow-up of plans, daily work and supervision.

management positions

management positions

Management in general and business management in particular rely on the implementation of four core functions:

Planning

It is to define objectives and build appropriate strategies and plans to reach decision-making, or to offer something new and positive in the final stages of the application of various administrative functions and processes.

Organization and coordination:

This is a process that regulates functions that aim to set appropriate rules, define the tasks and responsibilities that should be performed, according to specific steps, and thus ensure their coordination using administrative methods that help to distribute these tasks to the appropriate people in the work environment.

Driving and steering:

It is the application of the means to influence employees in a positive way by encouraging them to perform the tasks required of them, communicating and interacting, whether through training or assisting them in fulfilling their functions, and also by working to guide them in the proper ways that contribute to achieving the goals required efficiently.

Control :

It is a permanent follow-up to the work of the staff by looking at the results of the work, comparing what has been achieved realistically and what has been planned and still needs to be provided with tools and time to begin its actual implementation, and at the control stage the errors are discovered. Thus, they are reformed into private labor policies.

Relationship between management functions

The relationship between management functions is a complementary relationship (correlation, integration, interrelatedness) which is a rotation process with each other, ending only with the end of the company or management.

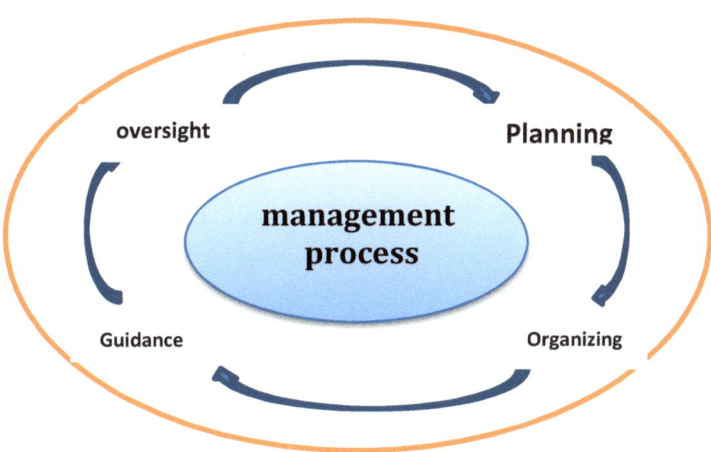

organizational structures

The importance of the organizational structure

Organizational structure is of great importance, summarized in the following:

1. The organizational structure helps the organization grow, work, because of clarity, focus.

2. The organizational structure regulates the flow of command and authority; every individual in the organization has a clear perception of his or her duties, of his or her legislators and of the reporting officer.
3. The organizational structure helps the organization analyze, understand its work, and know its current status.
4. The organizational structure arranges relations in the organization.
5. The organizational structure helps the organization reach its goals, and it is seen as one of the most important administrative tools in the organization.
6. The organizational structure contributes to clarifying the departments, administrative levels, departments, divisions and responsibilities assigned to each of them.
7. The organizational structure is an illustrative method that helps to study the history of the organization and its career development over certain periods of time.

8. The organizational structure helps the organization to detect and address errors in organization by detecting incorrect relationships and duplication of tasks.
9. The organizational structure contributes to the training of new staff members who join the organization by clarifying the organization's sections, indicating their location in the organization, and clarifying their superiors, their principals and the individuals to be contacted.

Types of organizational structures

The organizational structures in the organizations vary according to the objectives of the organization, the salary scale, the division of labor, and the most prominent types of organizational structures include the following:

Functional organizational structure

Where each employee in the organization is assigned to a single post, and their roles and responsibilities are clear; the functional organizational structure is determined by specialization, and the organization is divided into sections, for example: The Sales Section, the Accounting Section, and the Customer Service Section, it is important to note that the functional organizational structure has advantages, divided as follows.

Functional Regulatory Framework Highlights:

- The existence of a specialized principle in functions, departments, services, and the availability of experts and specialists in all fields.

The concise concepts of modern management   prof .*George Fayol* F-A-ALO

- To facilitate control, supervision of departments within the organization.
- To contribute to the resolution of the Organization's issues, by empowering the Chief Administrative Officer, and providing him with administrative, technical assistance.
- The ability to train employees in the tasks, and the work, as well as to enable supervisors to monitor the work.

the executive organizational structure

The authority in the executive organizational structure is central; that is, the authority is limited to the highest hierarchy of the organization, and there is only one president at the top of the organization, with the task of making decisions and orders, with lines of authority in the executive structure moving straight from top to bottom; Orders, instructions from presidents to subordinates flow and this structure is clear, simple, but there are some flaws.

These are the following points:

- Lack of cooperation and interdepartmental coordination.
- The need for specialists in work, and the separation of administrative, technical and professional functions.
- High-level officials have responsibilities beyond their capacity; they take charge of both administrative and substantive matters.

The consulting organizational structure

The consulting organizational structure integrates two types of structures; it includes the executive structure, the functional structure, and the authority has a unified central authority, such as the executive structure, in which the principle of specialization is used in the work, as well as the presence of experts, specialists who provide assistance, advice to heads, and administrators at work.

Advantages of the Regulatory Advisory Structure:

- It includes the principle of specialization in work.
- . Assist the experts, and the technicians of the chief administrators, thus enabling the presidents.
- Provide information to help decision-making.
- To develop and increase the expertise of the administrative authority.

Retinal organizational structure

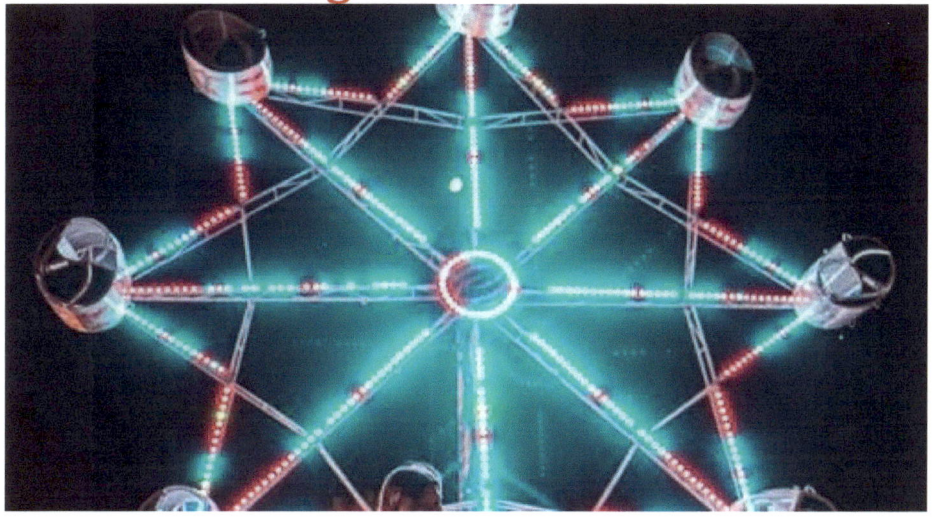

Retinal organizational structure

The organizational structure of the Retinal under the supervision of a small group of executives is the work done within the organization, the coordination of specific relationships with other organizations that undertake other operations, such as production, transport, marketing, etc. The advantages and disadvantages of the Retinal organizational structure are as follows:

Retinal organizational topology features:

- Possibility of using external resources from outside the Organization, which the Organization may need in its operations.
- To contribute to quality improvement through the use of specialized experts in this field.

Disadvantages of the Retinal organizational structure:

- Lack of direct control, owing to the inability of senior management to control operations directly within the Organization.

- Increased risk to the work of the Organization, owing to the possibility that contractors could not fulfill the agreed agreement between the parties.

The importance of the organizational structure

Organizational structure is of great importance, summarized in the following:

- The organizational structure helps the organization grow, and work; because of clarity, organization.
- The organizational structure regulates the flow of command and authority; every individual in the organization has a clear perception of his or her duties, of his or her legislators and of the reporting officer.
- The organizational structure helps the organization analyze and understand its work properly. And knowing the status quo.
- The organizational structure arranges relations in the organization.

- The organizational structure helps the organization reach its goals, and is seen as one of the most important administrative tools in the organization.
- The organizational structure contributes to clarifying the departments, administrative levels, departments, divisions and responsibilities assigned to each of them.
- The organizational structure is an illustrative method that helps to study the history of the organization and its career development over certain periods of time.
- The organizational structure helps the organization detect and correct any errors in organization, This is through the disclosure of improper relationships and duplication of tasks.
- The organizational structure contributes to the training of new staff members who join the organization by clarifying the organization's sections, indicating their location in the organization, and clarifying their superiors, principals and the individuals to be contacted.

The concise concepts of modern management   prof .*George Fayol* F-A-ALO

Forms of some organizational structures
These structures vary from one organization to another (depending on the size of the organization and its divisions).

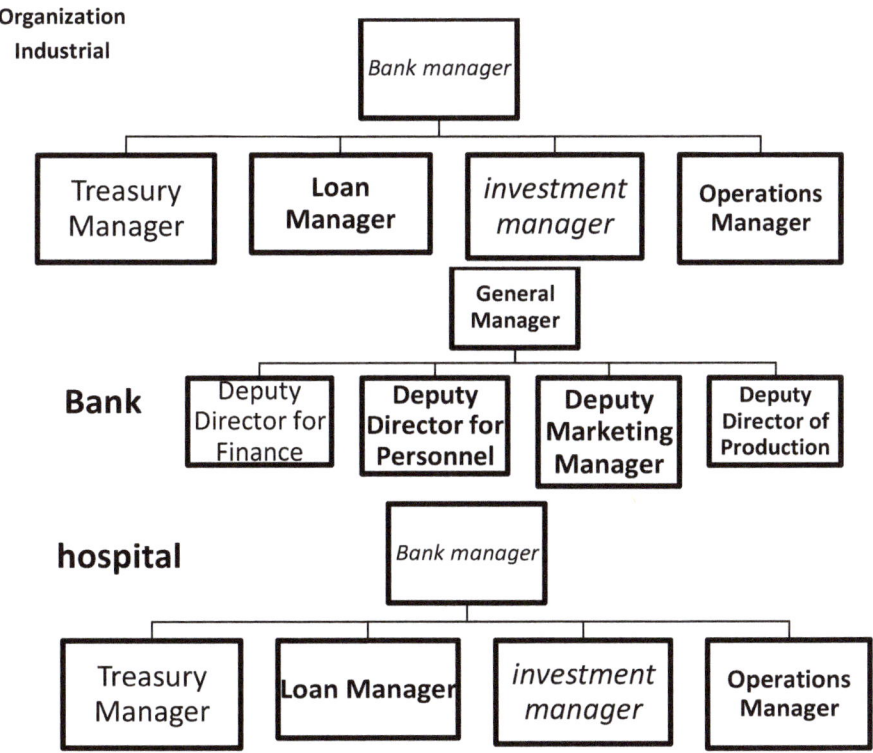

The concise concepts of modern management   prof .*George Fayol* F-A-ALO

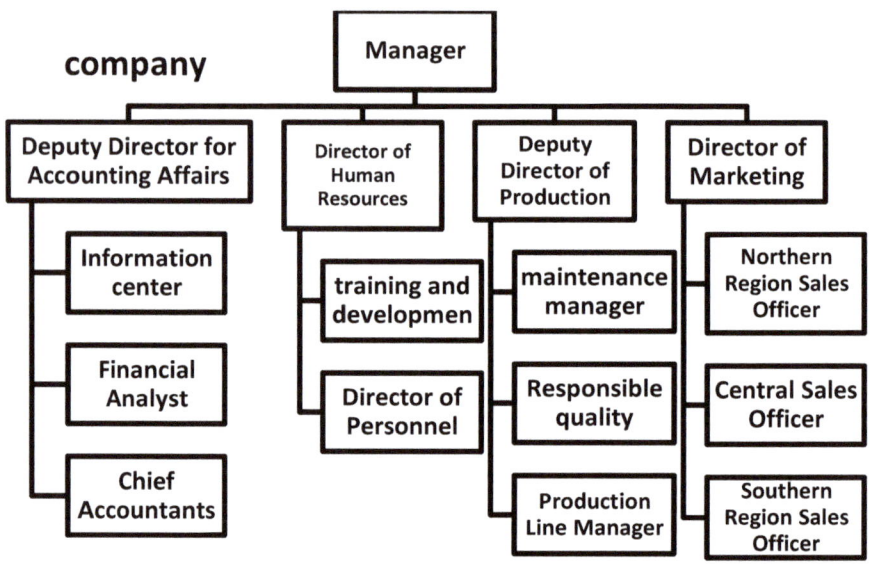

The concise concepts of modern management prof .*George Fayol* F-A-ALO

HUMAN RESOURCES

Human Resources:

It is the department that cares for employees in Facilities and companies, and focuses on their own tasks, by dividing activities that include training, hiring new employees, directing individuals, and providing their own benefits from financial and other benefits.

It is concerned with the management and training of staff as one of the most important assets of the work, and human resources are keen to follow up on the records of their recruitment.

Importance of human resources:

The importance of human resources can be summarized as follows:

- Achieving the strategic objectives of the organization.
- Managing staff and solving problems that arise between them.
- To train and support staff morale in order to increase staff productivity.
- Provide an enabling environment for action.

Human resources functions:

Some of the functions of human resources can be summarized as follows:

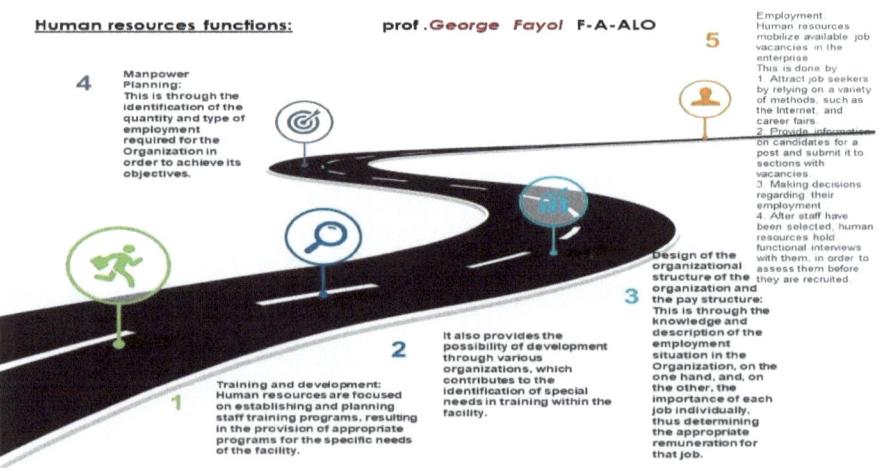

Human resources functions: prof .George Fayol F-A-ALO

5. Employment: Human resources mobilize available job vacancies in the enterprise. This is done by 1. Attract job seekers by relying on a variety of methods, such as the Internet, and career fairs. 2. Provide information on candidates for a post and submit it to sections with vacancies. 3. Making decisions regarding their employment 4. After staff have been selected, human resources hold functional interviews with them, in order to assess them before they are recruited.

4. Manpower Planning: This is through the identification of the quantity and type of employment required for the Organization in order to achieve its objectives.

3. Design of the organizational structure of the organization and the pay structure: This is through the knowledge and description of the employment situation in the Organization, on the one hand, and, on the other, the importance of each job individually, thus determining the appropriate remuneration for that job.

2. It also provides the possibility of development through various organizations, which contributes to the identification of special needs in training within the facility.

1. Training and development: Human resources are focused on establishing and planning staff training programs, resulting in the provision of appropriate programs for the specific needs of the facility.

Training and development:

Human resources are focused on establishing and planning staff training programs, resulting in the provision of appropriate programs for the specific needs of the facility. It also provides the possibility of development through various organizations, which contributes to the identification of special needs in training within the facility.

Design of the organizational structure of the organization and the pay structure:

This is through the knowledge and description of the employment situation in the Organization, on the one hand, and, on the other, the importance of each job individually, thus determining the appropriate remuneration for that job.

the Employment:

Human resources mobilize available job vacancies in the enterprise.

This is done by:

1. Attract job seekers by relying on a variety of methods, such as the Internet, and career fairs.
2. Provide information on candidates for a post and submit it to sections with vacancies.
3. Making decisions regarding their employment.
4. After staff have been selected, human resources hold functional interviews with them, in order to assess them before they are recruited.

The concise concepts of modern management   prof .*George Fayol* F-A-ALO

Manpower Planning:

This is through the identification of the quantity and type of employment required for the Organization in order to achieve its objectives.

Performance appraisal and employee motivation:

This is in order to measure the development or decline of staff performance, to identify the causes of the imbalance, to address them and to motivate staff by providing them with benefits.

Strengthening Employee Relations:

Within the employee's employment policies and laws, strengthening employee relations is the role of human resources, seeking to strengthen compliance with the property's laws and regulations, thus helping to maintain equal opportunity distribution among employees in a fair manner.

Payroll:

This is through the preparation of statements indicating employee benefits.

Other matters:

Leave to staff, study of employee complaints and prepare special reports according to which staff members are awarded an allowance, a grant, promotion or other matters.

Providing assistance to employees:

Human resources are responsible for overseeing the implementation of staff assistance programs, which contribute to helping staff to balance their normal and professional lives, and human resources personnel seek to implement savings programs and provide staff pensions.

Functions of the Human Resources Manager

Human Resources Manager's duties are all the activities that he applies within his or her competence in the organization or company, which contribute to the continued development of the business, among the most important of which are:

Achieve effective employee management:

It is the main task of the HR manager, seeking to achieve the appropriate management of all employees within the facility, so that he can easily identify the nature of their work, and guide them properly if they need any help in their tasks.

Performance appraisal:

It is a task for the HR manager to evaluate the performance of the staff by continuing their work, identifying errors if they are committed, helping them to overcome them, and ensuring that employees are actively involved and that they are fully performing the tasks required of them.

Developing the competencies of individuals:

A set of strategies followed by the HR manager associated with developing training and qualification programs that contribute to the development of the competencies of individuals in the organization and ensure that they achieve the best possible performance, so the HR manager is keen to select the best types of training courses to support staff efficiency.

Support for employee innovation:

One of the additional tasks of the Human Resources Manager that relies on working with employees to apply a range of innovative ideas, created by employees to contribute to adding new things to work, such as: Producing a new commodity that was not previously produced and other ideas.

Strengthening communication between management and staff:

Enhance communication between management and staff is a direct task of the HR manager, as he should strengthen communication between management and staff, especially if there are any requests the employee needs within the scope of the work, or in personal cases, such as sick leave and others.

Recruitment of new staff:

Is a key task for the HR manager; it is important to select and recruit new staff for a job, by testing, interviewing them, and ensuring that they are in line with the nature of the job they have offered, so that they can identify the appropriate employee to obtain the job vacancies in the organization.

The main roles of human resources, the human resources of the organization play three key roles

Strategic Participation:

It is the interaction and cooperation with the general management of the organization, through its participation in strategic decision-making, which ensures continuous work efficiency, as the human resources manager in some organizations is part of its board of directors, and he must present his suggestions in the search for competent employees, Especially for new projects that need to recruit new staff.

Application of employee rights:

An important human resource role, which seeks to maintain the application of employee rights, and to grant them all their privileges, and also to provide them with an appropriate working environment in conditions appropriate to their career range.

Management of Change and Development:

One of the relatively recent roles of human resources, which depends on supporting the planning role in institutions, is that the Human Resources Department in most organizations may change any policy that is applied incorrectly, or no longer achieve the desired results, especially if it is related to employees, Human resources seek to implement plans that provide all the needs that contribute to the continuity of development in the organization.

human resources policies

The Human Resources Department of the Enterprise implements a range of policies, including:

Balance Policy:

To work to harmonize management master plans with human resources plans, to achieve overall objectives in a balanced manner.

Performance Planning Policy:

Monitoring progress achieved in the different functional divisions by relying on a monthly performance measurement plan for each employee, and overall performance in each department of the organization or company.

Decision-making concepts and strategies

Definition of decision-making

Decision-making is defined as a process in which one of the available logical options is chosen, and when trying to make a good decision, man has to weigh the negatives and the pros of each option, and consider all alternative options. In order to make an effective decision, a person must be able to predict the results for each option as well, and on all of these elements the best option for a given situation is determined.

Steps for the decision-making process

A good way to make a decision is to follow a process that ensures that all relevant information is taken into account, and that each of the most likely results is taken into account, and is considered a (step-by-step) strategy that is crucial to achieving the decision-making process as follows:

- Identify the problem, opportunity, or challenge.
- create a range of solutions, or logical responses.
- To evaluate the costs and benefits, as well as the pros and cons associated with all options.
- Select the solution or response.
- Execute the selected option.
- Evaluate the impact of the decision, and adjust the course of action to requirements.

How to avoid making the wrong decision

The Director-General of an organization can avoid making the wrong decision by following the following strategies:

- Create multiple groups to study the issue.
- Training all employees on ethical conduct that suits the issue and work. Use of outside experts to review decision-making processes.
- Enter new members into the group, and move old members to another group.

Classification of decision-making

The decision-making process is classified according to three factors as follows:

The first classification is decision-making according to the level of decision, in terms of complexity, the importance of the decision itself, and the extent of the decision strategy.

Second Classification: Decision-making according to its general pattern, in terms of the extent to which others should be involved, and the circumstances in which participatory techniques may work better.

Third classification: Decision-making in terms of the conduct of the decision-making process, ranging from traditional, rational, to non-organized and self-directed.

The concise concepts of modern management   prof .George Fayol F-A-ALO

Wait for the second version of the book

www.ingramcontent.com/pod-product-compliance
Lightning Source LLC
Chambersburg PA
CBHW040244220526
45473CB00001B/361